Our World

Science Projects and Activities for Grades K-3

Written by Denise Bieniek

Illustrated by Bari Weisman

Troll Early Learning Activities

Troll Early Learning Activities is a classroom-tested series designed to provide time-pressured teachers with a wide range of theme-related projects and activities to enhance lesson plans and enrich the curriculum. Each book focuses on a different area of early childhood learning, from math and writing to art and science. Using a wide range of activities, each title in this series is chockful of innovative ideas, handy reproducible pages, puzzles and games, classroom projects, suggestions for bulletin boards and learning centers, and much more.

With highly interactive student projects and teacher suggestions that make learning fun, Troll Early Learning Activities is an invaluable classroom resource you'll turn to again and again. We hope you will enjoy using the worksheets and activities presented in these books. And we know your students will benefit from the dynamic, creative learning environment you have created!

Titles in this series:

Animal Friends: Projects and Activities for Grades K-3

Circle Time Fun: Projects and Activities for Grades Pre-K-2

Classroom Decorations: Ideas for a Creative Classroom

Early Literacy Skills: Projects and Activities for Grades K-3

Helping Hands: Small Motor Skills Projects and Activities

Hi, Neighbor! Projects and Activities About Our Community

Number Skills: Math Projects and Activities for Grades K-3

People of the World: Multicultural Projects and Activities

Our World: Science Projects and Activities for Grades K-3

Seasons and Holidays: Celebrations All Year Long

Story Time: Skill-Building Projects and Activities for Grades K-3

Time, Money, Measurement: Projects and Activities Across the Curriculum

Metric Conversion Chart		
1 inch = 2.54 cm	1 foot = .305 m	1 yard = .914 m
1 mile = 1.61 km	1 fluid ounce = 29.573 ml	1 cup = .24 l
1 pint = .473 l	1 teaspoon = 4.93 ml	1 tablespoon = 14.78 ml

Contents

Shapes in Nature

Materials:

- crayons or markers
- scissors
- construction paper
- glue

Directions:

1. Reproduce the art on pages 6–8. Display the art for the class and ask students to identify the geometric shapes they see in each object. Then ask them to name other objects having an identifiable shape found in nature or in human-constructed environments.

2. Talk about places where these objects may be found: natural environments, such as oceans, forests, rain forests, polar regions, deserts, mountains, rivers, and lakes; human-constructed environments such as cities, homes, and play-grounds. Ask each student to choose an environment he or she would like to create with construction paper.

3. Then have the children select pictures from the art repro-duced from pages 6–8 showing objects that could belong in their chosen environments. They may color the pictures, cut them out, and glue them to construction paper.

4. Students may wish to draw or cut out magazine pictures of other objects and animals to add to their construction-paper environments. Remind students that each picture should contain at least one recognizable geometric shape.

5. Display the construction-paper environments on the walls or bulletin board. Allow time for students to browse through them and observe the varied shapes that students chose.

Shapes in Nature

Shapes in Nature

Shapes in Nature

Name That Animal Game

Materials:

- two coated cardboard quart containers
- ruler
- pen
- tape
- construction paper
- scissors
- permanent marker
- glue

Directions:

1. Wash out and dry two coated cardboard quart containers. Cut the sloped top off each one.

2. To make die cubes from the containers, begin by cutting along the folds separating the sides.

3. Fold one panel on each container down. Trim off the remaining panels to the fold point. Then tape the folded panel to the opposite side, forming a cube, as shown.

4. Cover each side with construction paper by measuring and cutting individual squares of paper and gluing them to the sides of the cubes. Or cut strips of paper, apply glue to the backs, and wrap them around the cubes. Use clear tape to seal the seams.

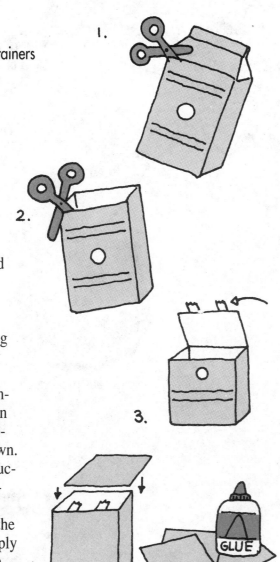

5. On each side of the first die, write the name of an animal covering (for example, fur, skin, scales, shell, feathers, quills). On each side of the other die, write the verb form of a characteristic animal movement (for example, swims, hops, runs, flies, slithers, climbs).

6. To play the game, have students sit in a circle. Choose one student to begin the game. That player rolls the dice in the center of the circle. After reading the two sides facing up, the player must name an animal to which both words apply. The other students must vote on whether the animal named fits the requirements. If a student cannot think of an animal having the characteristics shown on the dice, he or she is allowed to make up a name and try to fool the class.

7. Continue playing for as long as interest holds.

Body Parts Puzzle

Materials:

- crayons or markers
- scissors
- oaktag
- glue
- 9" x 12" cardboard sheets

Directions:

1. Reproduce the art on pages 11 and 12 once for each student. Have them color the pictures.

2. Demonstrate to the class how to mount the picture from page 11 onto a piece of oaktag and then cut it into pieces along the dotted lines.

3. Show the class how to mount the picture from page 12 onto a piece of 9" x 12" cardboard.

4. Explain to the class that the puzzle pieces show the interior features of the child in the puzzle and that the base picture shows the child's exterior. Demonstrate how to match the puzzle piece shapes to the base picture.

Body Parts Puzzle

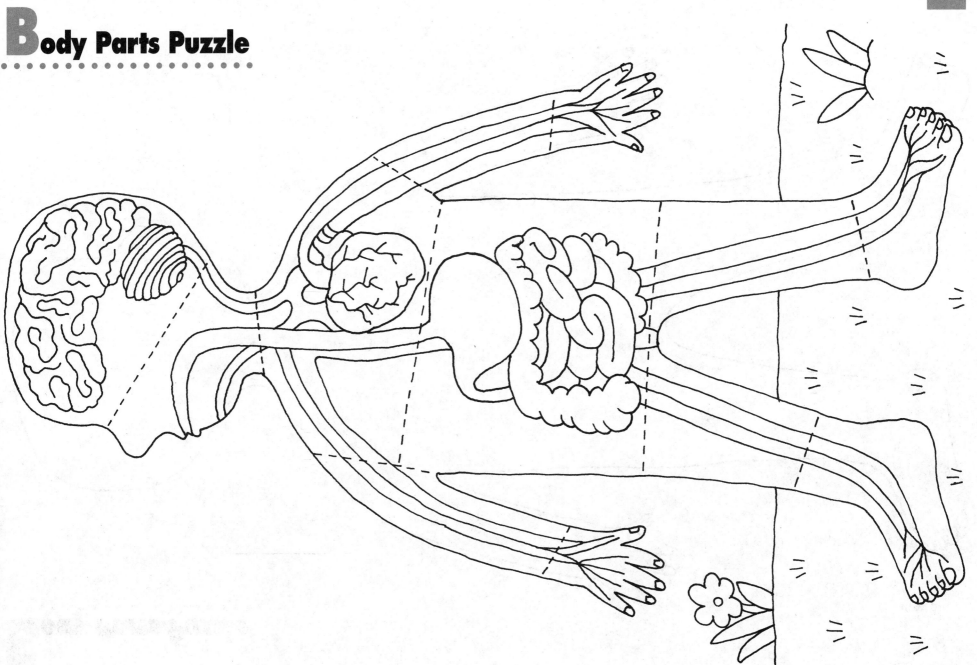

Body Parts Puzzle

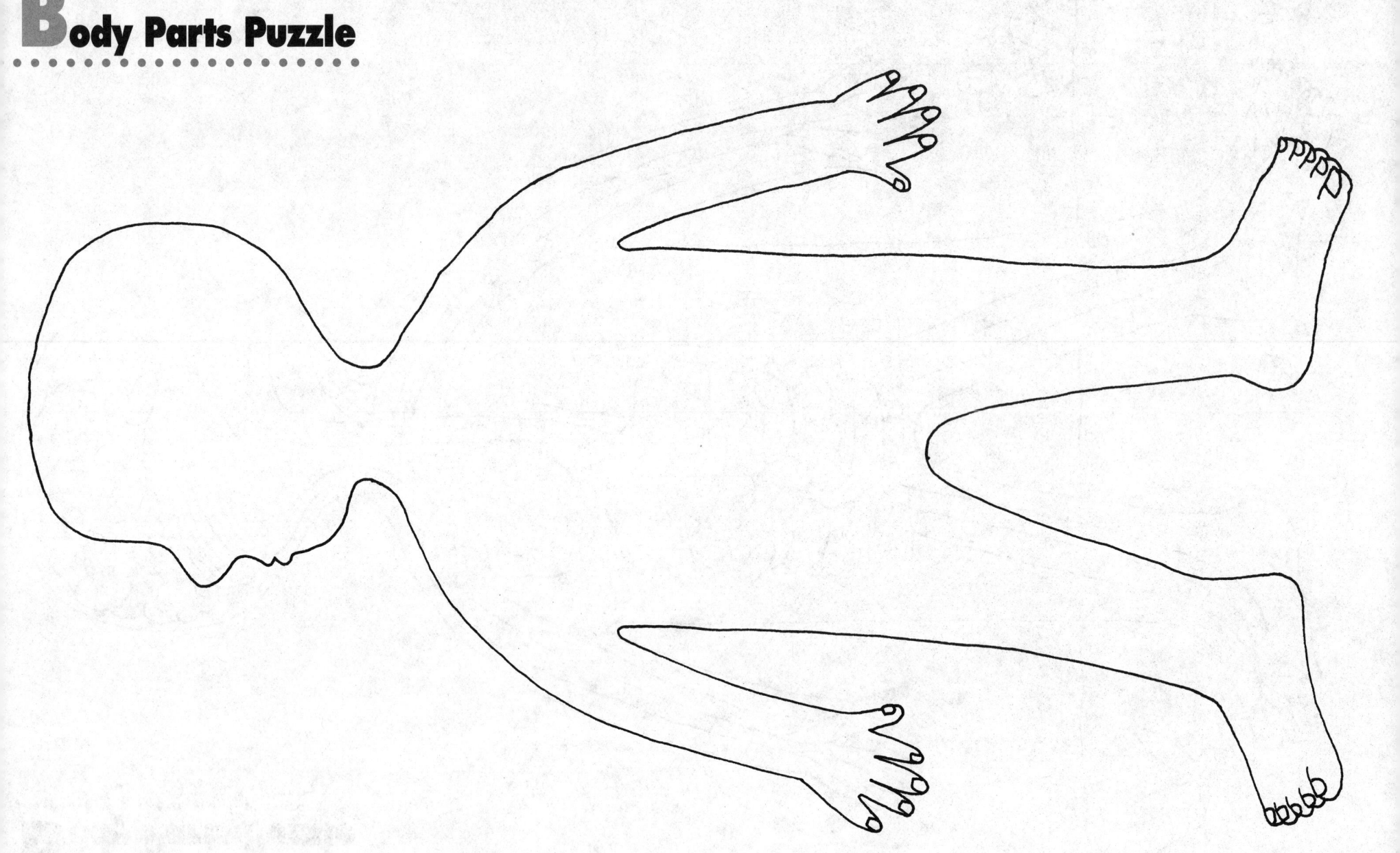

Five Senses Activity Boards

Materials:

- crayons or markers
- scissors
- large sheets of oaktag
- glue
- old magazines and workbooks
- hole puncher
- yarn
- transparent tape

Directions:

1. Reproduce the art on page 14 two times. Ask volunteers to color the pictures and cut them out.

2. Cut a sheet of oaktag in half. Down the left side of each half-sheet, glue a set of the five senses pictures.

3. Ask the class to look through old magazines and workbooks for pictures of objects that can been smelled, seen, heard, felt, and tasted. Choose five of these pictures, one illustrating each sense, and glue them in scrambled order down the right side of each half-sheet of oaktag.

4. Punch a hole below each picture on the left side. Then punch a hole below each picture on the right side.

5. Knot one end of a 20" length of yarn to each hole on the left side. Wrap a piece of tape around the free end of each yarn length.

6. To do the activity, tell students to decide which sense picture matches which illustration. To show a match, a student will place the free end of one of the yarn lengths into the hole below the correct picture on the right.

7. This activity may also be done as follows: On five half-sheets of oaktag, glue one sense picture on the left and five pictures from old magazines showing both appropriate and inappropriate matches on the right. Students must decide which picture or pictures match the sense being featured on that half-sheet of oaktag. Five yarn lengths can be tied into the hole below the sense picture so that students can place the free ends into the hole below the correct pictures.

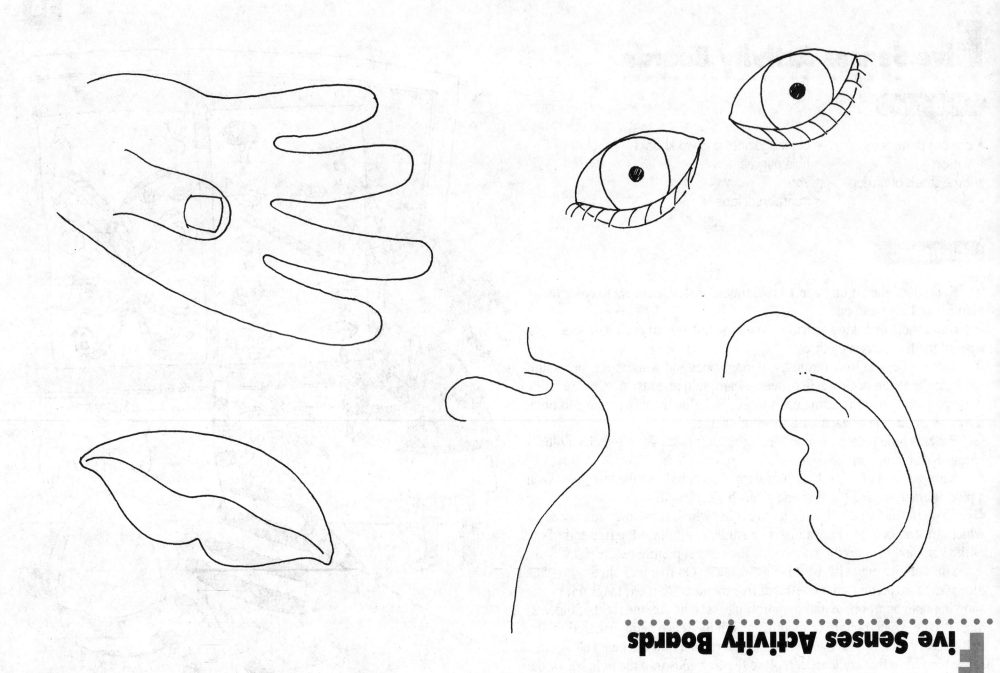

Five Senses Activity Boards

Nature Display

1. Take the class on a nature walk to observe and collect objects that catch their eye. Make sure each student has a small bag in which to put his or her collection.

2. While outside, discuss the texture of various objects. Talk about colors and their different shades. Point out the shapes and sounds of animals and plants.

3. After arriving back in the classroom, have the class sit in a circle. Ask students to speak briefly about one thing that interested them. They may also show their nature collections.

4. Display the chosen items on a table. Place magnifying glasses on the table as well. Write up activity cards presenting ways to use the materials on the display table. Each time an activity is completed, a student may write his or her name on the back of the activity card.

5. Some activity card ideas:

• Divide the items into categories. Find a friend and share your groupings with him or her. Then divide the items in each category into new and separate categories.

• Make rubbings. Lay an object under a piece of paper. Take the wrapping off a crayon and rub the crayon sideways on the paper over the object. Make more rubbings using other objects. Which objects are easiest to rub?

• Place all the rocks in size order from smallest to largest. Find a friend and show him or her your sequence.

• Make three sequence patterns using the materials on the table (for example, smallest to largest, roughest to smoothest, and brightest to palest in color). Find a friend and read your patterns to him or her.

6. Make sure all the materials students will need are near or on the display table. When students have completed all the activity cards, either make new cards or change the display.

What Belongs Where?

- crayons or markers
- scissors
- 9" x 18" pieces of oaktag
- glue
- old magazines and workbooks
- oaktag scraps
- clear contact paper
- small bag

Materials:

1. Reproduce the art on pages 17–19. Ask student volunteers to color the backgrounds.

2. Mount each background on a piece of oaktag, making sure to center it so that an even amount of oaktag shows on each side. Fold the oaktag edges along the sides of each background in toward the picture. These wings will help the backgrounds stand.

3. Have a class discussion about the suitability of each environment for various animals. For example, would a cow belong in a house as someone's pet? Would a bear get along with the other animals on a farm?

4. Distribute old magazines and workbooks to the class and ask students to cut out pictures of animals that belong in each of the three environments.

5. Mount the magazine pictures on oaktag and laminate.

6. Stand the three backgrounds next to each other on a table or the floor. Demonstrate how to play by holding up a picture of an animal and asking students where they think it belongs (for example, on a farm, in a house, or in the forest). Then choose a student to place it in the best environment.

7. Leave the activity where students will be able to play with it during free time. Keep animal pictures in a bag with the backgrounds.

What Belongs Where?

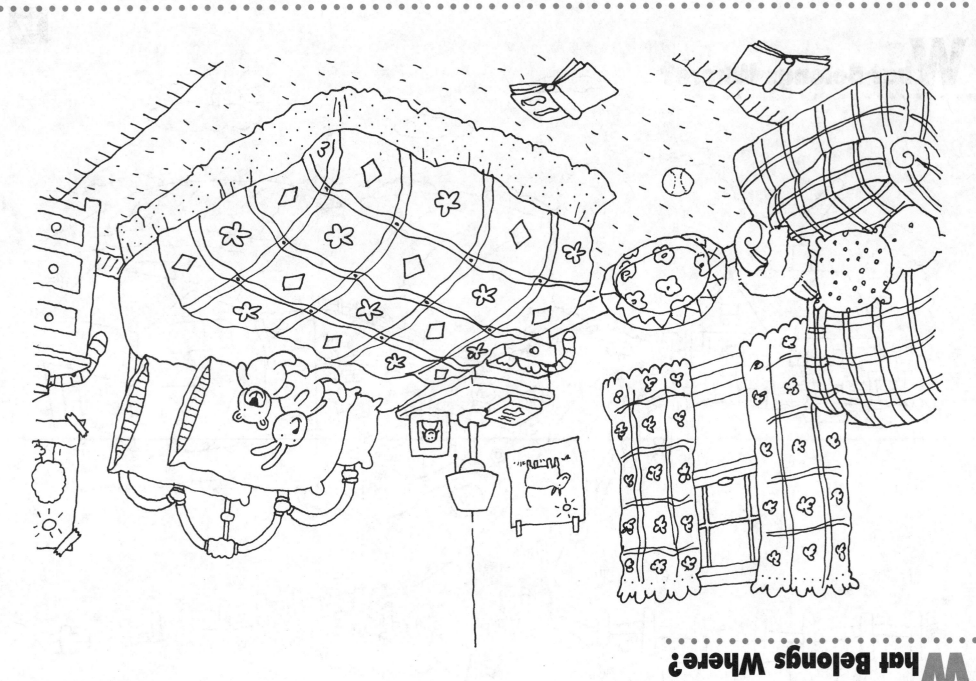

What Belongs Where?

Name _____

Supermarket Food Groups

Read the list of food items in the box below. Then write the name of each product under the name of the food group in which it belongs.

milk	ice cream	nuts	cheese
popcorn	hot dogs	cheese	red peppers
bread	eggs	potatoes	grapes
lettuce	carrots	butter	spaghetti
shrimp	steak	cereal	oatmeal
tuna	rice	yogurt	pudding
apples	chicken	orange juice	peanuts

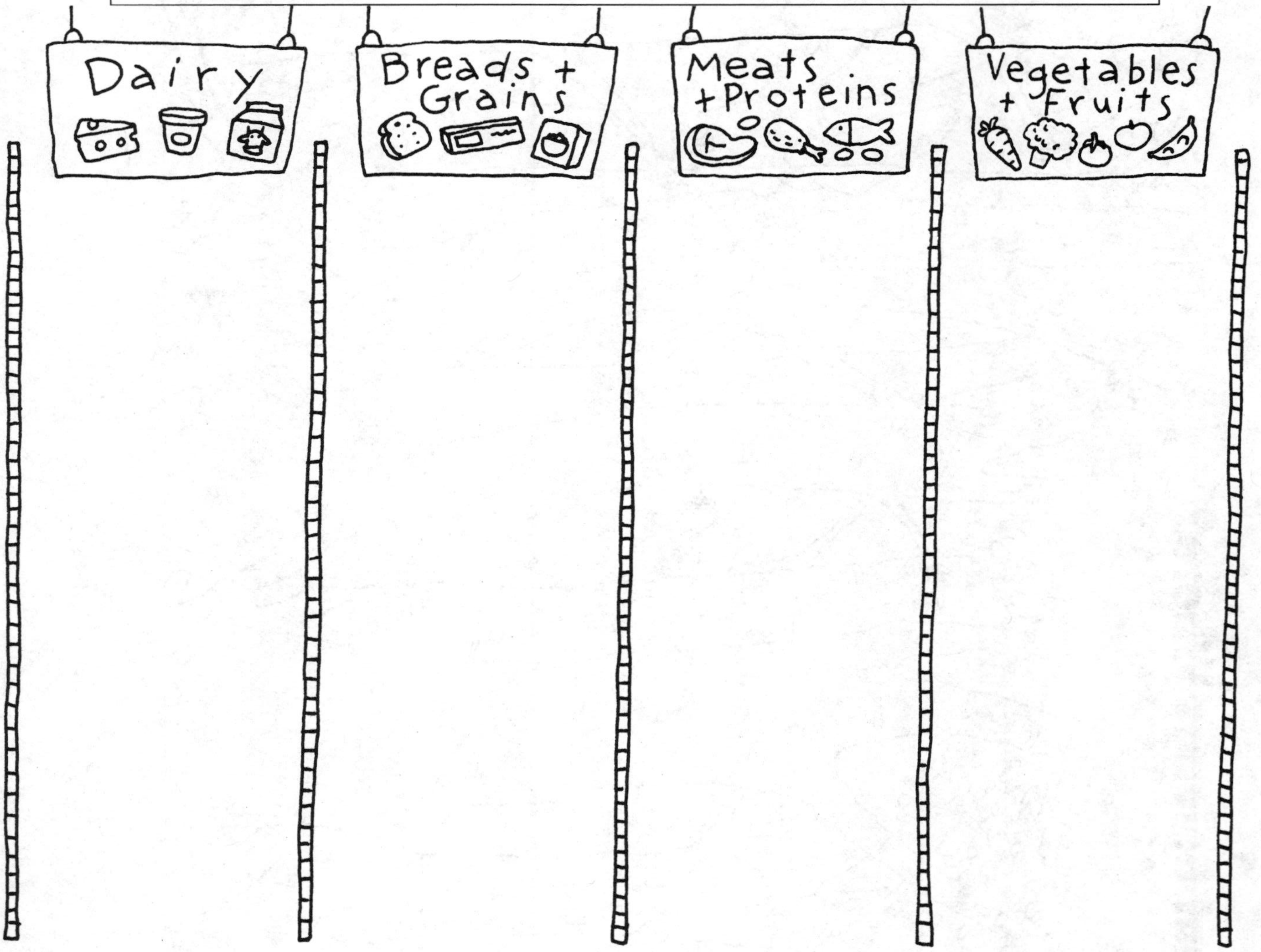

Dairy

Breads + Grains

Meats + Proteins

Vegetables + Fruits

Caterpillar Art

Materials:

- cardboard egg cartons
- scissors
- paints and paintbrushes
- construction paper scraps
- glue

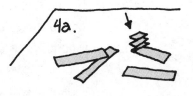

4. For legs, show students how to fold 1/4" x 3" strips of construction paper accordion-style. Then glue one end of each strip to the sides of each caterpillar. (Students may make as few legs or as many as they choose.)

5. Attach the caterpillars around the room—on the walls, on cabinets, hanging from the ceiling, and on the sides of desks.

6. Borrow books from the library about all kinds of caterpillars. Ask students to try to find the caterpillars that come closest to the ones they have made.

Directions:

1. Cut up egg cartons into smaller units of four cups each. Distribute a unit to each student.

2. Ask each student to choose a color (or colors) for his or her caterpillar. Have students paint only the outside of the carton unit.

3. When the paint is dry, hand out construction paper, scissors, and glue. Let students make faces for their caterpillars, as well as any markings they wish.

Creative Chrysalides

Materials:

- wallpaper paste
- bowls and water
- newspaper
- oval balloons
- sticks, about 12" long
- masking tape
- paints and paintbrushes
- thread
- clothespins
- string

Directions:

1. Combine wallpaper paste and water in small bowls. The mix should be thick but pourable. Make one bowl for every three students.

2. Ask volunteers to tear up strips of newspaper for the project. The strips should be approximately 1" x 6".

3. Give one balloon to each student. Ask each child to blow up the balloon carefully and make a knot at the opening.

4. Demonstrate how to cover a newspaper strip with the paste and run it through two fingers over the bowl to get off any excess paste. Then apply the strip to the balloon. Supervise students as they cover their balloons, making sure the strips lie as smooth as possible.

5. Make sure students cover their balloons with at least two complete layers of strips. To dry the balloons, students may hang them from their knotted ends with clothespins on a string hung across the room.

6. When the balloons are dry, give each student a sturdy stick approximately 12" long. Holding the sticks vertically, help students tape the knotted ends of their balloons to their sticks, covering the knot with tape.

7. Distribute paints and paintbrushes so students may paint their chrysalides.

8. Use thread to hang the chrysalides from the ceiling or the lights.

Potato-print Butterflies

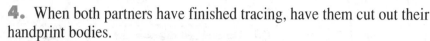

Materials:

- five potatoes
- knife
- crayons
- construction paper
- paints
- small bowls
- small buttons
- pipe cleaners
- thread or tape
- scissors

Directions:

1. Cut five potatoes in half. Use the knife to draw a simple abstract or geometric shape on each half. Then cut away the excess around the shape.

2. To make the butterfly body, ask each student to choose a piece of colored construction paper and a crayon. Have the children find partners and sit together in pairs.

3. While one partner places his or her hands on the paper, the other partner should trace around them. The hands should be placed so thumbs touch from top to bottom and the other fingers on each hand are as far from the thumbs as possible. Fingers may be kept together or spread out.

4. When both partners have finished tracing, have them cut out their handprint bodies.

5. Next, pour enough paint in a lid to cover the bottom. Place the small bowls in the center of the table and give one potato half to each pair of students. Have students at each table share the potato halves, making markings on their butterfly bodies as desired. Students may trade potatoes and paints with other tables. (Keep in mind that the paint will run out fairly quickly.)

6. When the paint is dry, students may wish to add features, such as eyes, antennae, and legs. Provide the children with buttons, pipe cleaners, and other decorating materials.

7. As the butterflies are finished, hang them from the ceiling or lights with thread.

The Changing Tree

Materials:

- blue, green, and brown construction paper
- stapler
- different shades of green tissue paper
- glue

Directions:

1. Staple blue construction paper to a bulletin board. Add a border of green construction paper along the bottom. To make the tree trunk, staple two sheets of brown construction paper side by side at the base of the board and two more side by side above them, just touching.

2. To make tree branches, ask students to tear strips of brown construction paper. Staple these to the board coming from the top part of the trunk and then branching off these main branches.

3. Have students make buds for the branches of the tree by tearing squares of green tissue paper and crumpling them until they are fairly small. Glue these buds to the branches of the tree on the left side, as shown.

4. Tell the children to make small leaves for the branches in the middle of the tree. These leaves may be torn from sheets of green tissue paper and then glued to the branches in the middle of the tree.

5. Tear large leaves from green tissue paper and attach them to the branches on the right side of the tree.

6. Students can "read" the tree from left to right telling a story of how a tree grows again each year from the spring to the end of summer. If possible, add the art from pages 21–23 to the tree. Place caterpillars on the left side of the tree, chrysalides in the center, and butterflies on the right side.

7. Title the bulletin board "The Changing Tree."

Nature Report

• • • • • • • •

Mr. Johnson's class went on a nature walk and submitted the following article to the school newspaper about it. Circle all the mistakes you find and write the correct words on another piece of paper.

Nature Walk
by Class 209

Yesterday our class went outside for a nature walk. We seen all kinds of different things. Yasmine saw a bird feeding her baby worms in there nest. Bobby saw a cat sunning itself in a window of a house nearby. Sara watched an aunt carry a peice of bread bigger than itself to an anthill! Tony was scared when a squirel ran right in front of him and jumped up onto a fence. We all laughed about it, including Tony.

Mr. Johnson says there are many things to see if we keep are eyes open and observe quietly. Sumtimes animals are startled if we are too loud. We tried standing still and watching to see what wood happen by the woods near the school. A rabbit came out and hopped around for a minut or two, but Craig sneezed and it ran away. The rabbit had really long back feet and powerfull legs to help it jump away.

Back in our classroom, we discussed what we saw outside. Our walk was fun, and we decided to do it again when the season changes to see if anythin different will happen.

Ladybug Matchups

Materials:

- crayons or markers
- scissors
- white oaktag
- Velcro (with the sticky back)
- pocket folder

Directions:

1. Reproduce the ladybug art on page 27 once and cut it out.

2. Trace the ladybug body and wings ten times onto white oaktag. Cut out the shapes.

3. Stick a piece of hard Velcro onto the center of the left and right sides of each ladybug body front.

4. On each pair of wings, draw or write about two things that belong together. For example, for younger students, simple and complex designs to match are good ways to practice visual discrimination skills. For older students, you may wish to write a math equation on one wing and the answer on the other. Other ideas for pairs of wings: patterns, number to dots, word to picture, phonics, shadow to object, animal to environment.

5. The same thing can be done with phonics: on each of a pair of wings, draw a picture of an object beginning with a particular sound (such as a ball and a bat), and then the matching letter or letters on a ladybug body. Students will be asked to attach the wings to the body showing the letter or letters representing the correct sound.

6. Attach a piece of soft Velcro onto the center backs of all the left and right wings.

7. To play, show students how to find matching pairs and attach them onto a ladybug body.

8. Store the activity in a folder with pockets. Place the activity folder on a bookshelf or in the science center for students to use during free time.

Ladybug Matchups

Chinese Fans

Materials:

- craft sticks
- glue
- white construction paper
- watercolor paints and paintbrushes
- scissors

Directions:

1. Brainstorm with the class about wind. Write all the children's comments on a chalkboard and discuss.

2. Categorize the comments under headings the students create. For example, one category may be about how the wind helps people: transporting seeds, propelling boats with sails, creating power through windmills, bringing cooler air, and keeping kites aloft.

3. Explain to the class that sometimes the air is very still. One way to get it moving again is by using a fan. Hand-held Chinese fans can be very delicate and have beautiful scenes painted on the front of them.

4. To make fans with the class, distribute six craft sticks to each student. Demonstrate how to layer the sticks so just one end of the sticks overlap and the other ends fan out. Glue the overlapped ends together.

5. When the glue is dry, lay the fan on white construction paper. Trace the shape of the fan onto the paper, making the shape 1" bigger all around. Cut out the shape.

6. Encourage the students to paint a scene carefully on one side of their fans.

7. Squeeze a line of glue onto each craft stick and gently press the paper fan shape onto the sticks.

8. When the glue has dried, the fans are ready to be used.

Swimmy Cake

Materials:

- boxed cake mix and ingredients
- frosting
- mixing bowl
- mixer
- spatula
- plastic knives
- plates and forks
- rectangular cake pan

Directions:

1. Read *Swimmy* by Leo Lionni (Knopf, 1963) to the class. Talk about how Swimmy was able to save the school of fish by getting them to work together so they resembled a big fish.

2. Have a class discussion about the food chain in the sea. Explain to the children that smaller animals eat plants, medium animals eat the smaller, and the larger animals eat the medium and small animals.

3. Make a fish-shaped cake in honor of Swimmy. Assemble all necessary ingredients and materials and mix the cake, following the directions on the package. Bake the cake in a rectangular pan.

4. When the cake has cooled, find the center of one of the shorter sides and mark it with a small knife cut. Cut from this spot to a point on the upper long edge of the cake, about 4" in from the marked side. Repeat for the lower edge. Use the cutout triangles to make a larger triangle for Swimmy's tail, placing a point at the center spot the cuts were made from.

5. Ask several students to work together to frost the cake. To make Swimmy's scales, zigzag the knife from top to bottom. Use frosting to make a fin for Swimmy. Use a piece of candy for Swimmy's eye. Enjoy!

Best Books About Weather

Share some or all of the following books about weather with the class. Place the books in the reading or science center for students to review during free time.

Cloudy with a Chance of Meatballs by Judi Barrett (Atheneum, 1978)

The Cloud Book by Tomie dePaola (Holiday, 1975)

Bringing the Rain to Kapiti Plain by Verna Aardema (Dial, 1981)

City in the Winter by Eleanor Schick (Macmillan, 1970)

Thunderstorm by Mary Szilagyi (Bradbury Press, 1985)

The Secret Language of Snow by Terry Tempest Williams and Ted Major (Pantheon, 1984)

Weather Watch by Adam Ford (Lothrop, 1982)

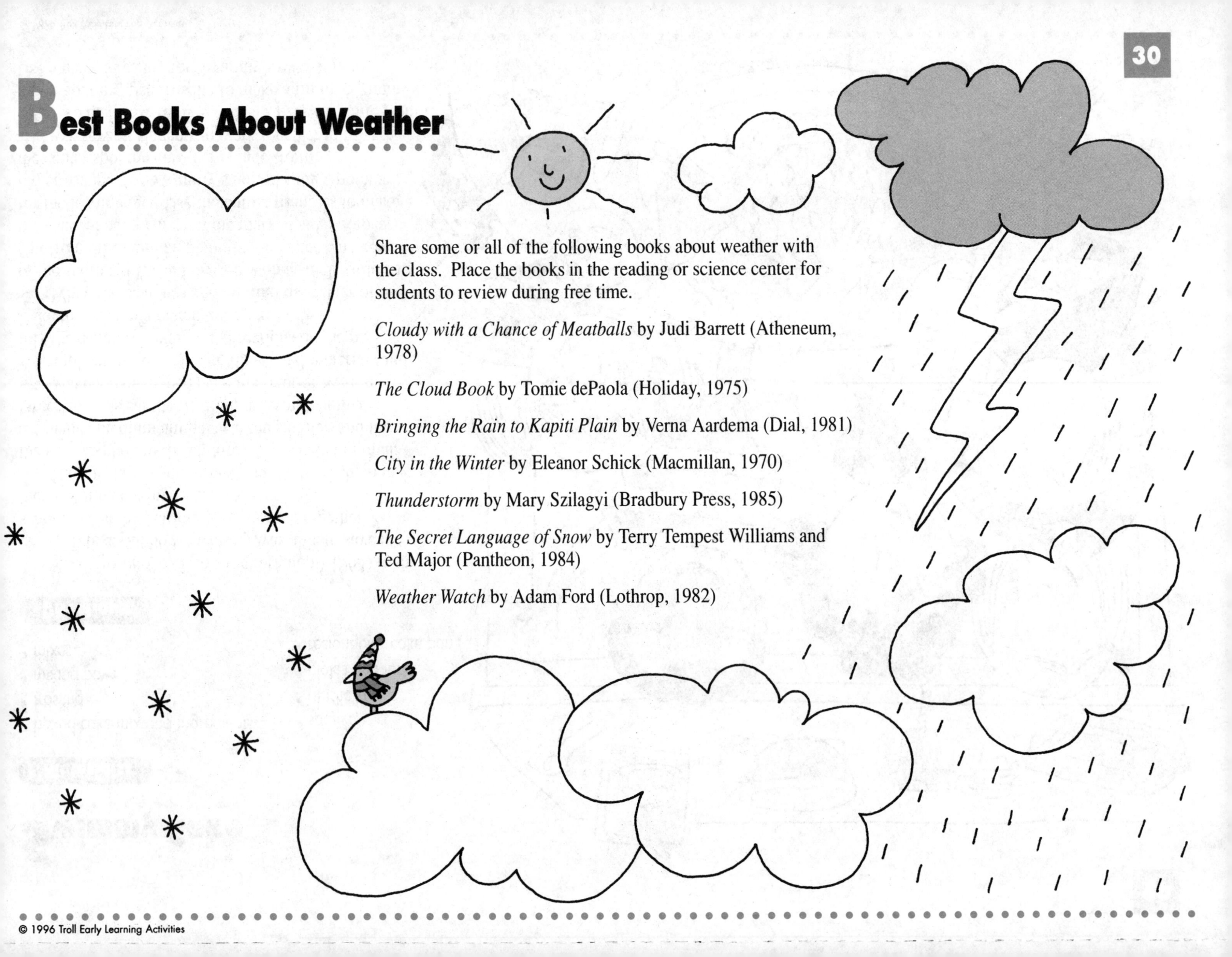

"The Turnip" Flannel Board

Once upon a time, a farmer went out to his garden to harvest his turnips. He saw one turnip that was ready to be pulled out of the ground. The farmer pulled and pulled on the turnip, but no matter how hard he tried, he could not pull it out of the ground.

The farmer called to his wife to come help him. She ran out of the house to the garden. The farmer pulled on the turnip and the wife pulled on the farmer. They pulled and pulled, but no matter how hard they tried, they could not pull that turnip out of the ground.

Next, the farmer's wife called to the horse to help them. The farmer pulled on the turnip, the wife pulled on the farmer, and the horse pulled on the wife. They pulled and pulled, but no matter how hard they tried, they could not pull that turnip out of the ground.

The horse called to the cow to help them. The farmer pulled on the turnip, the wife pulled on the farmer, the horse pulled on the wife, and the cow pulled on the horse. They pulled and pulled, but no matter how hard they tried, they could not pull that turnip out of the ground.

The cow called to the dog to help them. The farmer pulled on the turnip, the wife pulled on the farmer, the horse pulled on the wife, the cow pulled on the horse, and the dog pulled on the cow. They pulled and pulled, but no matter how hard they tried, they could not pull that turnip out of the ground.

The dog called to the cat to help them. The farmer pulled on the turnip, the wife pulled on the farmer, the horse pulled on the wife, the cow pulled on the horse, the dog pulled on the cow, and the cat pulled on the dog. They pulled and pulled, but no matter how hard they tried, they could not pull that turnip out of the ground.

The cat called to the bird to help them. Everyone turned to stare at the cat. If they couldn't pull the turnip from the ground, how was a tiny thing like a bird going to help? But still they tried. The farmer pulled the turnip, the wife pulled the farmer, the horse pulled the wife, the cow pulled the horse, the dog pulled the cow, the cat pulled the dog, and the bird pulled the cat. They pulled and pulled and pulled and pulled. And all of a sudden, the turnip came out of the ground!

"The Turnip" Flannel Board

Reproduce the story characters on this page and page 33. Color the figures and cut them out. Then glue flannel scraps to the back of each figure. Add the figures to the flannel board as the characters appear in the story. Later, let the children use the figures to recreate the story or make up stories of their own.

"The Turnip" Flannel Board

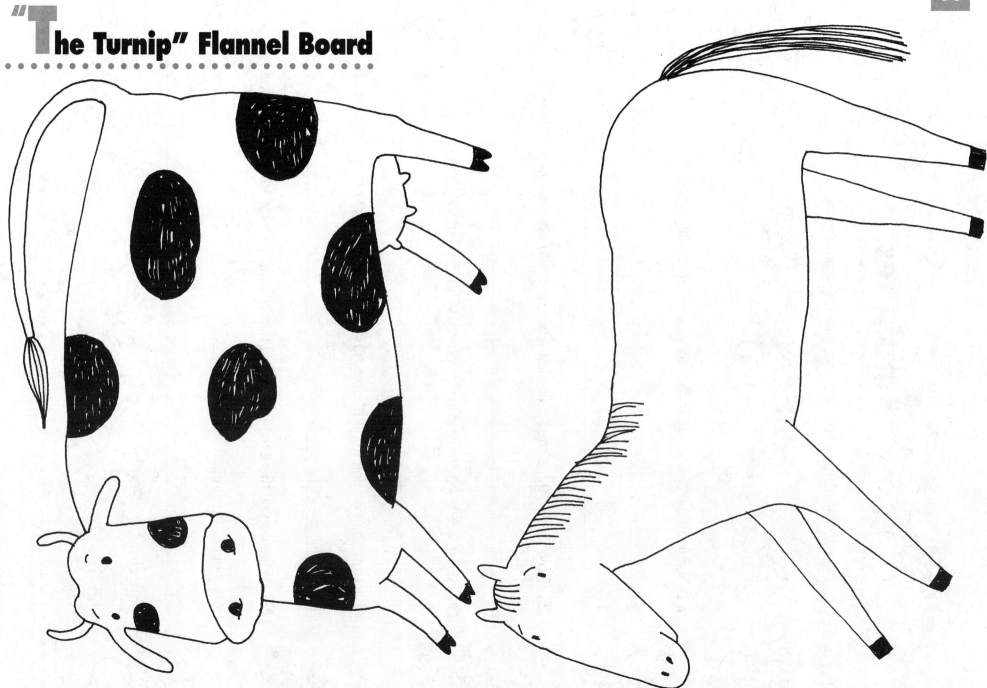

Name _____

Turnip Test

After hearing the story "The Turnip," try to answer the questions below.

1. Name all the characters in the story in the order they appeared.

_____

_____

2. How do you think the farmer felt when he could not pull up the turnip?

_____

3. What would you have done if you could not pull up the turnip?

_____

4. How long do you think it took to finally pull the turnip out of the ground?

_____

5. What do you think the farmer and his wife did with the turnip after it was

pulled out of the ground? _____

_____

Animals on Parade

1. Borrow books from the library about animals from around the world. Be sure to include books containing information about physical characteristics, how animals defend themselves, what they eat, where they live, and any special features or adaptations they have developed.

2. Give each student time to choose one animal in which he or she is interested. Ask students to do "KWL" charts. This type of chart is divided into three columns. The first column is called "What I *K*now"; the second column is called "What I *W*ant to Learn"; the third column is called "What I *L*earned."

3. Above the column headings, have the children write the names of the animals they have chosen. Students may then begin filling in the first two columns. Students may use the library books for research. They may also interview people who have knowledge of their chosen animals, such as zookeepers or people who live in the same regions as the chosen animals.

4. When each child has completed the third column in his or her chart, he or she should be ready to give a presentation to the class about the animal. Give students a range of options for their reports: video, lecture, demonstration, costume, and so on.

5. Encourage students to prepare models of their animals. Show them how to make a model by drawing the animal on butcher paper, tracing the shape again on butcher paper, then cutting out both figures.

6. Provide the children with crayons, markers, paint, or chalk. They may add collage materials as well.

7. Next, demonstrate to the class how to staple the edges of the figure together, leaving about 6" open. Students can then stuff their animal shapes with crumpled newspaper and staple the openings closed.

8. These models can be displayed around the room with small index cards attached telling visitors relevant information about the animals.

Mother Nature Statues

1. Brainstorm with the class on the topic of nature. Write down students' comments on a chalkboard. Categorize the ideas to help the class think about the qualities of nature and ways of expressing them.

2. Discuss the ideas mentioned. Then ask the class if anyone has ever heard of the concept of "Mother Nature." Ask students what they think "her" purpose is.

3. Inform the class that they will be making Mother Nature statues. The images will be their interpretations of what they think Mother Nature might look like. Remind students that Mother Nature may be a person, an animal, or anything from their imagination. Students should be prepared to explain how they made their statues and why they used the materials they did.

4. Layout materials for students to use for their statues:

recycled containers and other clean garbage

collage materials

fabric

old magazine pictures

different types of paper

papier mâché

modeling clay

5. When the statues are finished, display them around the room. Place index cards next to the statues telling how the image was made and what special symbolism or significance the materials used has in relation to the concept of nature. For example, a student may use green paper shreds for the hair to symbolize plant life, which is the basis of life for humans. Or a student may use all recycled materials to show the importance of recycling used materials instead of burning them or filling dumps with garbage unnecessarily.

6. Invite the class to browse through the display. Hold a question-and-answer session after the showing. Students may ask questions and make comments about each other's versions of Mother Nature. If desired, invite other classes to see the display, or place the statues in a showcase where everyone can see the students' creations.

Nature Words Jumble

Find the words listed in the box below in the word search puzzle. The words may appear forward, backward, up, down, or diagonally.

```
E C O C O A Y P S H E L E F S U T I O N
G T A I N R O C K S G N I N L K C T I B
R E S E A D I O B A B Y D L G A S T T H
T O I S E N O V O T K P O C T D N I U A
H R S S N U T A U N R P O N M E E A S C
D N E A R T H Q U A K E F O L E M H A S
A I H R N E E S L L E H S A E S I C O R
Y A T O E I U D O L C V E C A N F T E O
P H N O E Q A P V N A A L V D G A S O T
A C Y F R E K T H M Y G O L O C E Y A I
M D S U T C A C N O I A R N R Y T M L E
O O L A O A R N U T U N O O G I E O O O
O T P A L E V J C O D O F C B S A U C S
M F O I A V A H S L A M I N A E T S N E
Y N H V I G Y S E A T M O H T E A R H T
D A P R D Y T H G I L I G H T N I N G O
```

tree	moon	forest	habitat	sun
river	food chain	jungle	mountain	pond
tundra	sea shells	ocean	seed	desert
rain	ecology	cactus	rocks	photosynthesis
cloud	animals	lava	lightning	earthquake

Spinning Webs

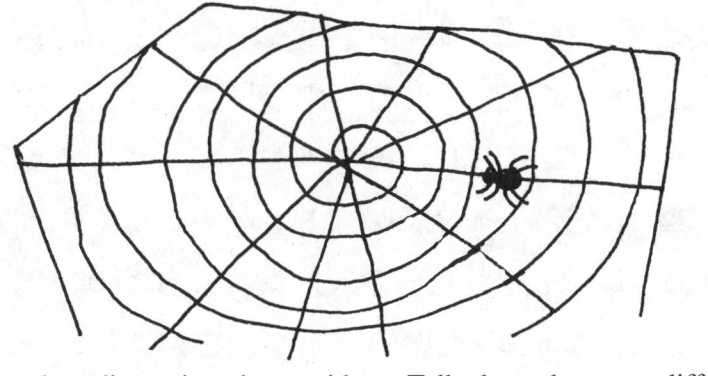

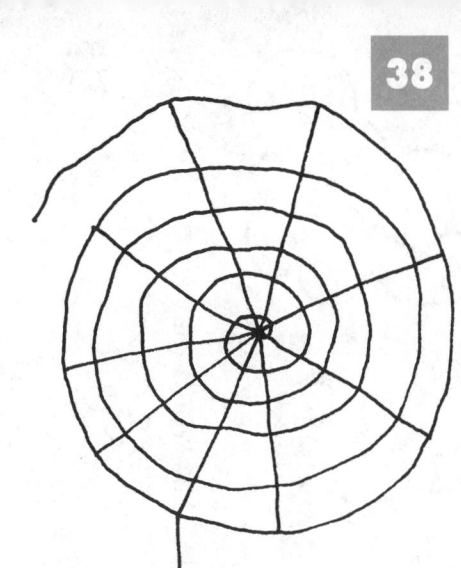

1. Have a class discussion about spiders. Talk about the many different kinds of spiders and about how some spiders are helpful to humans, while others are not (and some can even be dangerous).

2. Explain to the children how a spider spins a web. The spider lets out a length of silk from its body to attach from one support to another. Then the spider lets out more threads to form the frame of the web. The spider continues letting out threads until it has formed a web that looks somewhat like a wheel with many spokes.

3. Ask if anyone knows why a spider builds a web. Discuss the fact that insects get caught in the web because the web is naturally sticky. The spider does not get stuck in its own web because of a natural secretion on its feet.

4. To show students the intricacy of a web, try to find one in the classroom or another part of the school. Blow a light dusting of baby powder onto the web to show its lines and patterns.

5. If possible, place a spider in a container with a meshed top. Make sure that the container is secure and that the spider cannot escape. Let students observe how the spider slowly begins to build its web until the web becomes stronger.

6. As an extension activity, write words *spider web* on a chalkboard. Ask the class to see how many words they can think of that can be made from the letters in these two words (e.g., *red*, *peer*, *sew*, *dew*).

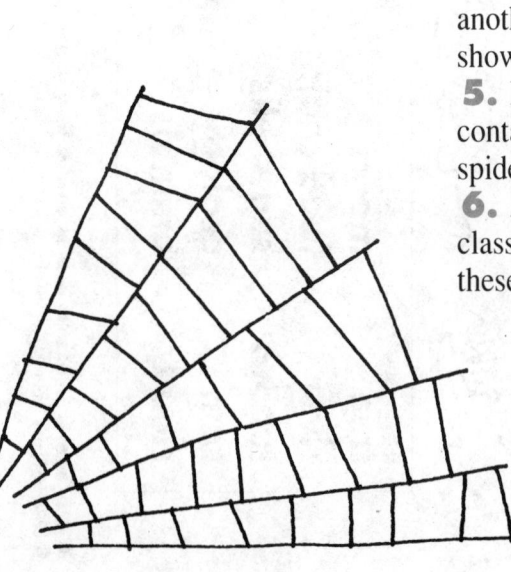

Name _____

Connect the even-numbered dots in the picture below in order to see why this bug is running away.

Bug Trouble

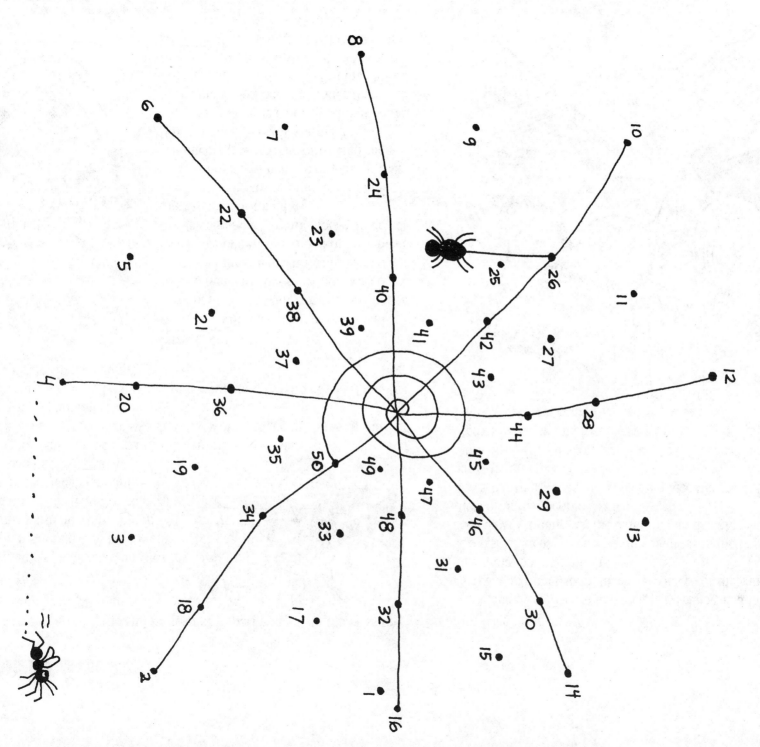

Simple Science

Perform some or all of these simple science experiments with the class to illustrate some basic principles.

Salt Makers

1. Tell the class that salt comes from deposits in mountains. When rivers and streams wash down the mountains, the salt is carried into the ocean. That is why the ocean contains salt water instead of fresh water.

2. Show how salt can be separated by filling a small dark bowl with water and then adding a tablespoon of salt to the water. Place the bowl in sunlight until the water evaporates.

3. Ask volunteers to tell why the salt has remained in the bowl. (Only the water evaporates in the sunlight.)

Heat It Up

1. Have volunteers cover two small cardboard boxes with construction paper. Ask students to cover one box with black paper and the other with white paper.

2. Place one of the same kind of object inside each box. Try to choose an object that is made of metal.

3. Put the boxes in direct sunlight for several hours. When the time is up, ask volunteers to touch the objects in each box. Which object is warmer?

4. Ask if anyone can explain why objects in the black box become hotter than objects in the white box. Tell the children that dark colors absorb light and heat, while light colors reflect light and heat.

Sun Bleaching

1. Place pieces of white paper, newspaper, and facsimile paper outside each day in direct sunlight. Place pieces of the same types of paper inside on a table, out of sunlight.

2. Ask students to observe the changes in the paper that is placed outside each day. Explain that the sunlight can discolor the paper just as it discolors (tans or burns) people's skin.

3. After two weeks of exposure, place the paper from outside next to the paper that remained inside. Explain to students that some paper became more discolored than others because each sheet is made from a different type of paper and includes different chemicals. These chemicals react differently in direct sunlight.

Plants All Around

1. Ask volunteers to name different types of plants with which they are familiar. Write the children's comments on a large piece of oaktag.

2. After everyone who wishes to has added to the discussion, assign one of the plants on the list to each child to research.

3. Allow students time to go to the library to look up information about their plants in books or encyclopedias. If possible, take a class trip to a nursery or invite a landscaper or botanist to the classroom to discuss plants.

4. After students have completed their research, ask them to draw pictures of their plants on 12" x 18" construction paper. Have each student write the name of the plant at the top of the paper and three facts about the plant at the bottom.

5. Attach the plants to a bulletin board under the title "Plants All Around."

Name _____

Plant Parts

Look at the drawing below. On the lines provided, write in the name of each part of the plant. For help, look at the words in the box at the bottom of this page.

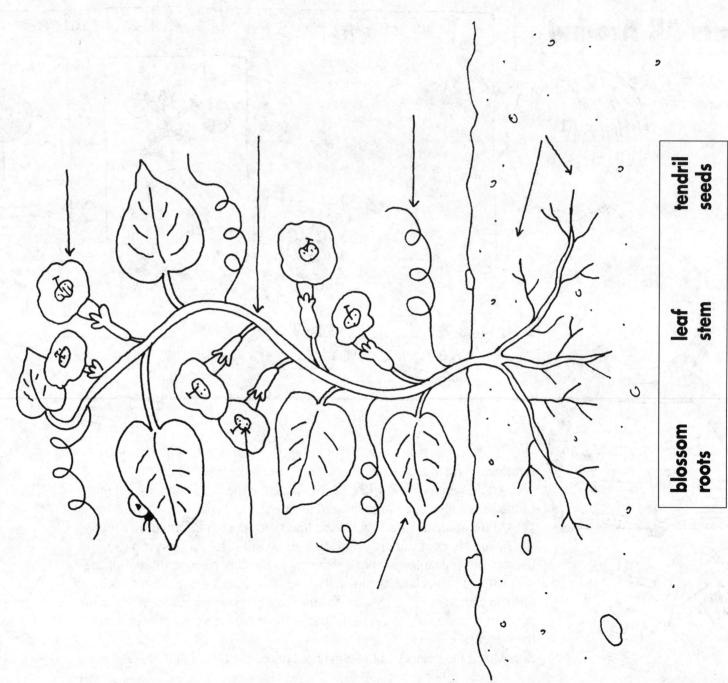

blossom	**leaf**	**tendril**
roots	**stem**	**seeds**

Name _____

Plant Facts

Read each of the statements below. On the lines provided, write a "T" if the statement is true. Write an "F" if the statement is false.

1. A plant needs a gallon of water each day. ____

2. Plants need sunlight in order to grow. ____

3. You can eat the roots of some plants. ____

4. You cannot eat the seeds of any plant. ____

5. The leaves of a plant make food for it. ____

6. The stem of a plant holds it in place. ____

7. The seeds of a plant grow into new plants. ____

8. Cotton comes from a plant. ____

9. Most plants need soil in order to grow. ____

10. Lettuce is a type of plant. ____

My Own Zoo File-Folder Game

Materials:

- crayons or markers
- scissors
- glue
- letter-sized file folder
- oaktag
- clear contact paper
- playing pieces
- envelope
- number cube

Directions:

1. Reproduce the game board on pages 45–46 once. Color the game board, cut it out, and glue it to the inside of a letter-sized file folder, as shown.

2. Reproduce the "How to Play" instructions below once. Glue them to the front of the file folder.

3. Reproduce the game cards on pages 47–48 four times. If desired, ask volunteers to color the game cards. Mount the game cards on oaktag, laminate them, and cut them out.

4. On the back of each game card, write the category of animal to which each animal belongs: mammal, bird, amphibian, reptile, fish, or insect.

5. Make four playing pieces by cutting out four different-colored squares of oaktag. Or use a penny, nickel, dime, and quarter for playing pieces.

6. Glue an envelope to the back of the file folder. Store the game cards, playing pieces, and a number cube or die inside.

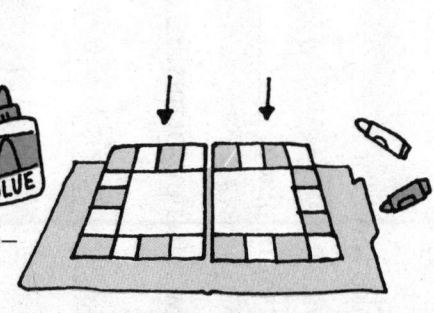

How to Play
(for 2–4 players)

1. Players place their playing pieces on "Start." Place the game cards in a pile with the pictures faceup.

2. Each player rolls the number cube once. The player with the highest number goes first.

3. The first player rolls the number cube and moves his or her piece clockwise around the board the appropriate number of spaces. The player then follows the directions on the space on which he or she has landed.

4. If a player lands on a space that has an animal on it, he or she draws a game card from the top of the pile. The player looks at the picture, tells which type of animal it is, and turns the card over to reveal the answer. If he or she is correct, the player may keep the card. If a player is incorrect, the card is placed in a discard pile.

5. Play continues clockwise around the game board. Each player must try to collect two of each type of animal (12 cards total). If the game cards are used up, players should shuffle the discard pile and continue playing.

6. The first player to collect two of each type of animal is the winner.

My Own Zoo File-Folder Game

My Own Zoo File-Folder Game

My Own Zoo File-Folder Game

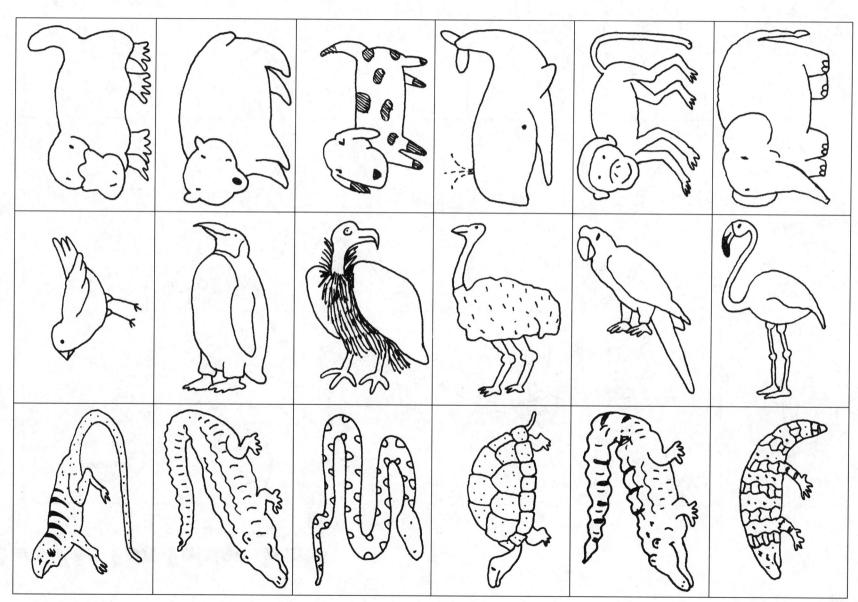

Mammal

Bird

Reptile

My Own Zoo File-Folder Game

Insect

Fish

Amphibian

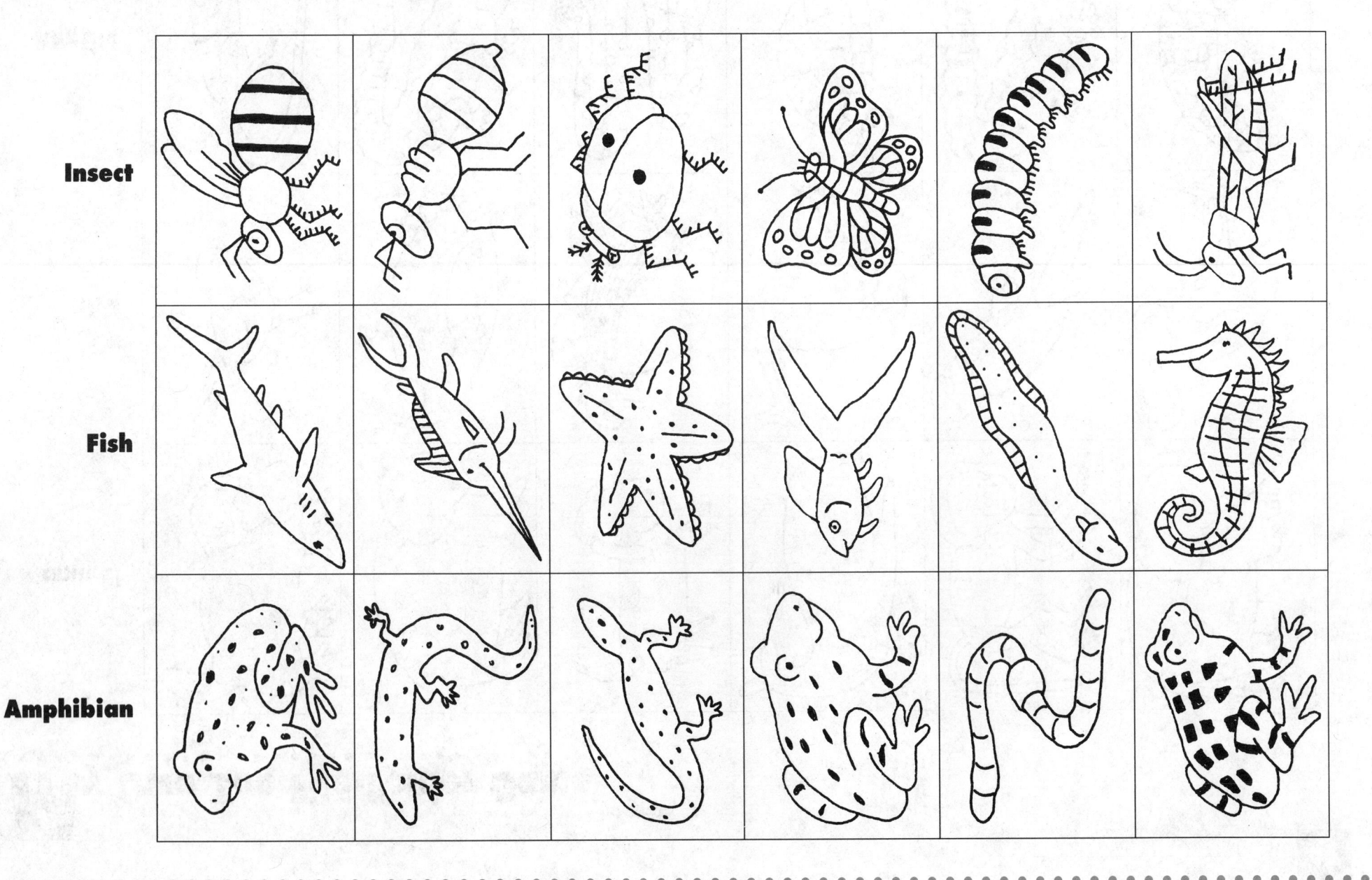

Endangered Animals Books

Materials:

- crayons or markers
- glue
- oaktag
- scissors
- lined paper
- hole puncher
- yarn or thread

Directions:

1. Introduce the concept of endangered species to the class. Explain that certain kinds of animals have become extinct because of hunting or changes in their habitats caused by human activities. Animals may also decrease in numbers naturally, due to extreme weather conditions or lack of food. Species that drastically decrease in number over a short period of time are often called endangered. Tell the class that people and organizations take steps when possible to prevent endangered animals from dying out.

2. Ask each student to choose one of the figures on pages 50–52 as the subject for an endangered animal book. Reproduce the selected animal once for each child. Have students color the animals, mount them on oaktag, and cut them out.

3. Help students research their endangered animals. Ask each child to find out some information about his or her animal, such as:

type of animal (mammal, reptile, etc.)	foods
physical appearance	habits
natural habitat	reasons endangered

4. Allow students library time to research their animals. Encourage the children to take notes while doing their research.

5. When a child is satisfied with his or her research, have him or her use the selected animal figure as a template to make pages for the book. Show students how to trace each figure onto lined paper as many times as necessary for each report.

6. Have each student cut out the animal shape from the lined paper. Ask each child to cut out two shapes from oaktag to make front and back covers for his or her book.

7. Once students have written their reports, show each child how to place the covers and pages together in order and punch two or three holes along the top or left side of the figure.

8. Place yarn or thread through the holes and tie together to bind each book. Encourage the children to think of titles for their books.

9. Ask volunteers to read their books aloud to the rest of the class. Then place the books in the reading or science center for everyone to see.

Endangered Animals Books

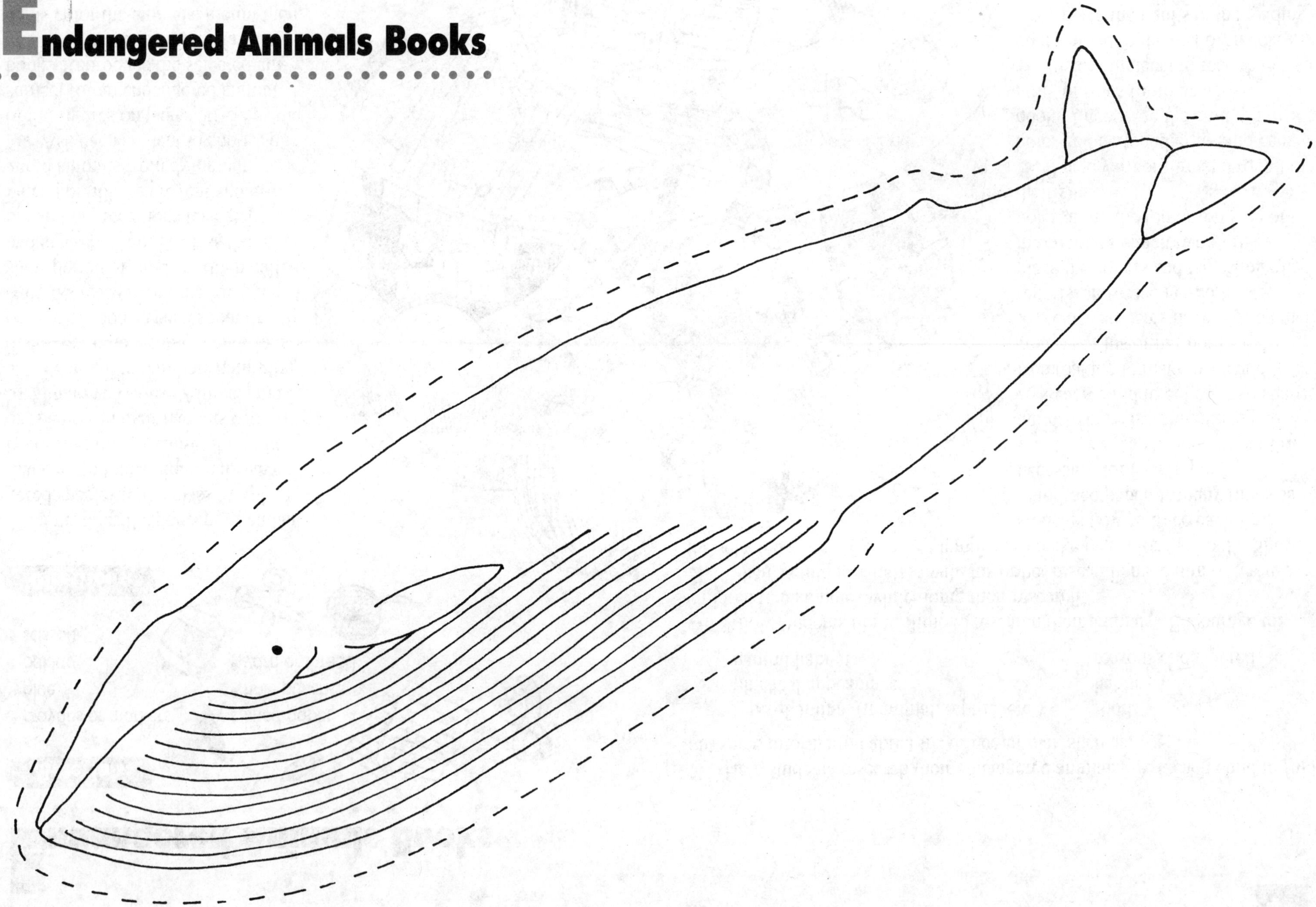

ndangered Animals Books

Name _____

Animal Habitats
••••••••••

A **habitat** is the kind of place where a person or animal lives.
Write down the natural habitat for each of the animals listed below. Use the words in the box if
you need help.

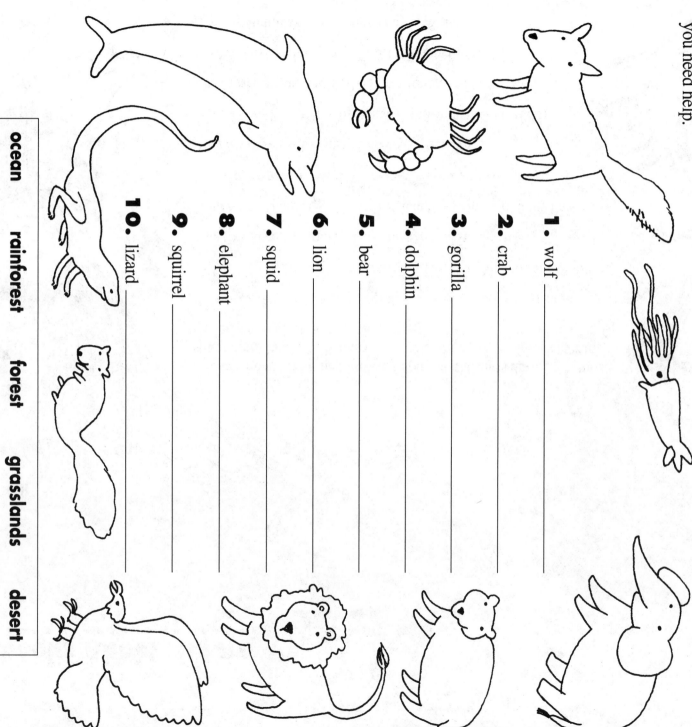

1. wolf _____

2. crab _____

3. gorilla _____

4. dolphin _____

5. bear _____

6. lion _____

7. squid _____

8. elephant _____

9. squirrel _____

10. lizard _____

| ocean | rainforest | forest | grasslands | desert |

Best Books About Nature

Read some or all of the following books to the class during a nature study unit. Place the books in the class library or reading center for students to look at during free time.

When Dad Cuts Down the Chestnut Tree by Pam Ayres (Knopf, 1988)

If You Are a Hunter of Fossils by Byrd Baylor (Macmillan, 1980)

The Tiny Seed by Eric Carle (Picture Book Studio, 1991)

Sometimes Things Change by Patricia Eastman (Childrens Press, 1983)

Natural History by M. B. Goffstein (Farrar Straus Giroux, 1979)

Animals at Night by Sharon Peters (Troll, 1983)

Once There Was a Tree by Natalia Romanova (Dial, 1985)

The Lorax by Dr. Seuss (Random House, 1971)

Do Not Disturb by Nancy Tafuri (Greenwillow, 1987)

Eyes by Judith Worthy (Doubleday, 1989)

Name _____

Nature Hunt

Play naturalist. See how many interesting natural forms you can find near your house. Check off each of the items below if you see it. On the lines provided, describe each item in more detail.

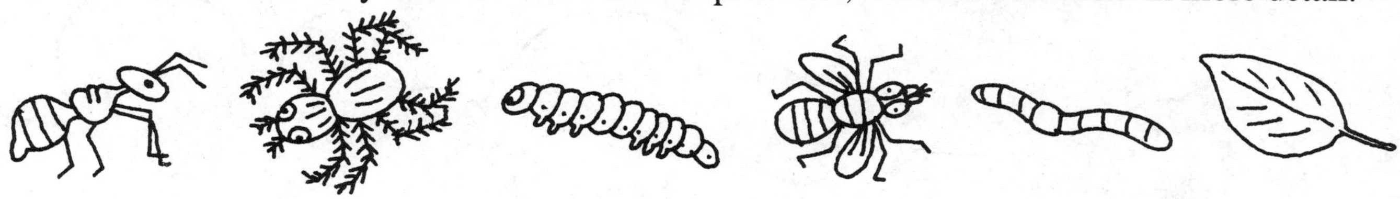

☐ ant _____

☐ spider _____

☐ caterpillar _____

☐ fly _____

☐ worm _____

☐ bird _____

☐ nest _____

☐ flower _____

☐ weed _____

☐ moss _____

☐ leaf _____

☐ seedling _____

Weather Word Search

Name _____

Try to find the hidden weather words in the puzzle below. The words may be written forward, backward, up, or down.

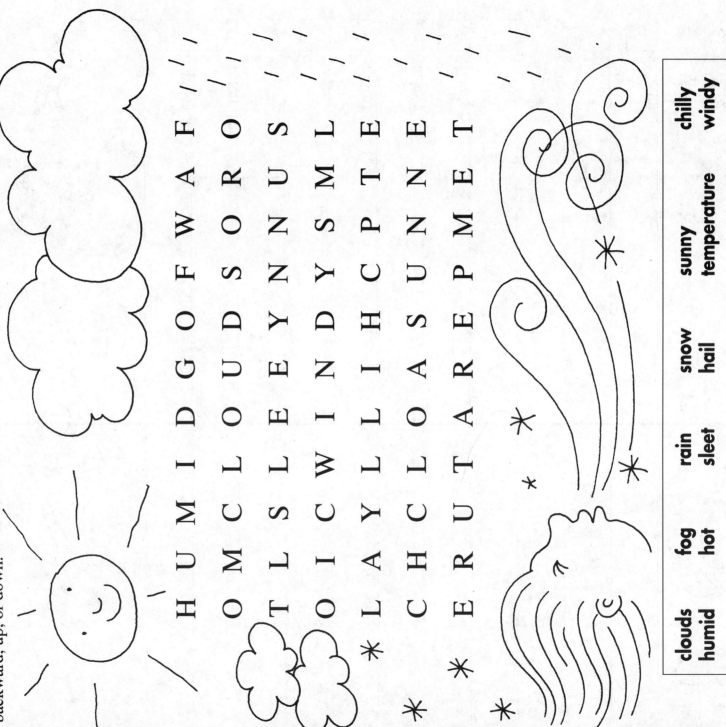

H U M I D G O F W A F

O M C L O U D S O R O

T L S L E E Y N N U S

O I C W I N D Y S M L

* L A Y L L I H C P T E

C H C L O A S U N N E

* E R U T A R E P M E T

clouds	fog	rain	snow	sunny	chilly
humid	hot	sleet	hail	temperature	windy

Traveling Light

1. Have a class discussion about light. Set up some simple experiments to show how light travels. Begin by lighting a candle and holding it near several objects to show how the candlelight illuminates all around the candle. Then shine a flashlight on the same objects. Help students understand that the light from the flashlight only travels in a straight line.

2. Ask volunteers to tell what kinds of objects light can travel through (clear glass, cellophane, sheer fabrics, etc.). Then hold up various materials to the window. See if students can predict which materials are transparent (light shines through clearly), which are translucent (light shines through, but less clearly), and which ones are opaque (light does not shine through).

3. Help the children understand how light can cast shadows. Take the class outside on a sunny day. Show students how their bodies (which are opaque) block the sunlight. Tell the children that their shadows are the result of this blocking. Experiment with shadows at the beginning, middle, and end of the school day to show how the shape and size of the shadow changes with the movement of the sun, which is the light source.

Pressed Flower Art

Materials:

- flowers
- 4" x 4" pieces of clear contact paper
- oaktag
- scissors
- glue
- tape

Directions:

1. Ask each child to bring in several flowers. Flowers may be found at home in gardens, in supermarkets, or at nurseries.

2. Gently tear the petals from each flower. Place the petals in a large pile in the center of a table.

3. Give each child two 4" x 4" pieces of clear contact paper. Let four children at a time go up to the table and choose several petals to use to make a collage.

4. Show each child how to remove the backing from the piece of contact paper and then carefully arrange the petals on the sticky side.

5. Help each child remove the backing from the second piece of contact paper and place it on top of the petals, sticky-side-down.

6. If desired, let the children use oaktag to make frames for their pressed flower collages. Cut 1/2" x 4" strips and glue one to each side of the collage. Attach the collages to classroom windows so that light shines through.

Name _____

Moon Watch

Fill in the dates on the calendar below. Each night, draw a picture of what the moon looks like in the sky. On the back of this sheet, write down notes about how the sky looks, where the moon is located in the sky, or what type of weather has occurred.

Month _____

Sun	Mon	Tues	Wed	Thurs	Fri	Sat

Name _____

How Many Moons?

Fill in the chart below. Use an encyclopedia or a book about space if you need help.

Planet	Number of moons
Mercury	
Venus	
Earth	
Mars	
Jupiter	
Saturn	
Uranus	
Neptune	
Pluto	

If You Can't Take the Heat . . .

the white is cooler.

1. Show the class how the sun's heat affects different things in different ways. Begin by explaining that the sun is the source of life for almost all living things on Earth (for example, humans need sun for vitamin D, and plants need sunlight in order to grow).

2. Choose several objects from the room for the experiment. For example, you may pick a wooden block, some aluminum foil, and a plastic toy. Place the objects in direct sunlight for about an hour.

3. Ask volunteers to feel each object and describe its temperature. Which objects absorbed the most heat? Which objects absorbed the least heat?

4. To illustrate why people in warm climates wear light-colored clothing, place a piece of white fabric and a piece of black fabric in direct sunlight for about an hour. After students have had the opportunity to feel each fabric, explain that the white fabric reflects the sunlight, which keeps it cooler. The dark fabric absorbs the light, which makes the fabric warm.

Magnetic Force

1. With the class perform some simple experiments with magnets. Begin by demonstrating how magnets attract metal objects, such as nails, paper clips, and foil.

2. See if a strong magnet will attract objects through other objects. Place a nail inside a glass jar. Hold a strong magnet to the outside of the jar. What happens?

3. Next, pour water inside the jar. Hold the magnet up to the outside of the jar to see if the magnet still works.

4. Then try wrapping a piece of photocopier paper around the ends of the magnet. Hold the magnet near a nail. What happens?

5. Hold the magnet up to a thin piece of wood. Place a nail on the other side of the wood. What happens?

6. Ask students to predict which materials the magnet can work through. Write the predictions down a large piece of oaktag. Then perform the experiments to see which predictions are correct.

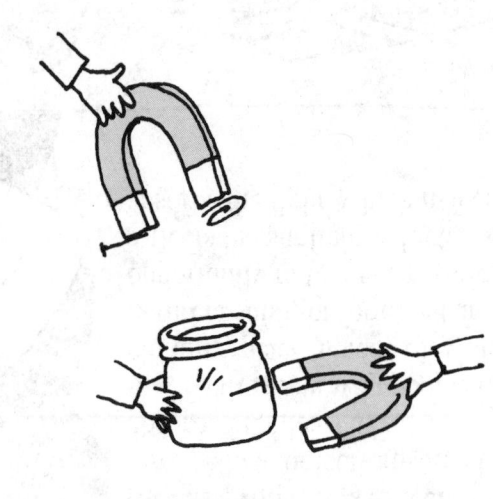
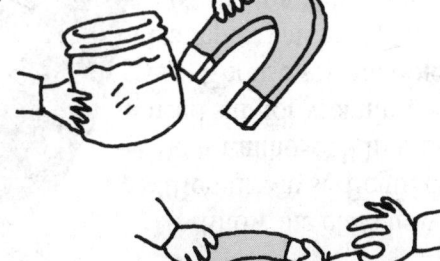

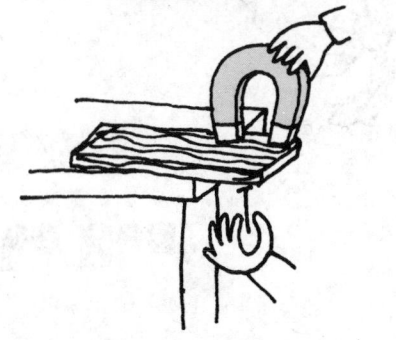

Material	Prediction
cloth	yes
Stone	no
Cardboard	yes

- AWARD -

Presented to _____
for Super Science Skills.

Teacher _____   Date _____

Answers

page 20

DAIRY

milk
ice cream
eggs
cheese
butter
yogurt
pudding

BREADS & GRAINS

popcorn
bread
rice
cereal
spaghetti
oatmeal

MEATS & PROTEINS

shrimp
tuna
hot dogs
steak
chicken
peanuts
nuts

VEGETABLES & FRUITS

lettuce
apples
carrots
grapes
potatoes
orange juice
red peppers

page 25

Nature Walk
by Class 209

Yesterday our class went outside for a nature walk. We seen all kinds of different things. Yasmine saw a bird feeding her baby worms in there nest. Bobby saw a cat sunning itself in a window of a house nearby. Sara watched an aunt carry a peice of bread bigger than itself to an anthill! Tony was scared when a squirel ran right in front of him and jumped up onto a fence. We all laughed about it, including Tony.

Mr. Johnson says there are many things to see if we keep are eyes open and observe quietly. Sumtimes animals are startled if we are too loud. We tried standing still and watching to see what wood happen by the woods near the school. A rabbit came out and hopped around for a minut or two, but Craig sneezed and it ran away. The rabbit had really long back feet and powerfull legs to help it jump away.

Back in our classroom, we discussed what we saw outside. Our walk was fun, and we decided to do it again when the season changes to see if anythin diferent will happen.

page 34

1. farmer, turnip, wife, horse, cow, dog, cat, bird
2-5. Answers will vary.

page 37

```
E C O C O A Y P S H E L E F S U T I O N
G T A I N R O C K S G N I N L K C T I B
R E S E A D I O B A B Y D L G A S T T H
T O I S E N O V O T K P O C T D N I U A
H R S S N U T A U N R P O N M E E A S C
D N E A R T H Q U A K E F O L E M H A S
A I H R N E E S L L E H S A E S I C O R
Y A T O E I U D U O L C V E C A N F T E
P H N O E Q A P V N A A L V D G A S O T
A C Y F R E K T H M V G O L O C E Y A I
M D S U T C A C N O N I A R N R Y T M L
M O O L A O A R N U T U N O O G I E O O
O O T P A L E V J C O D O F C B S A U C
M F O I A V A H S L A M I N A E T S N E
Y N H V I G Y S E A T M O H T E A R H T
D A P R D Y T H G I L I G H T N I N G O
```

page 39

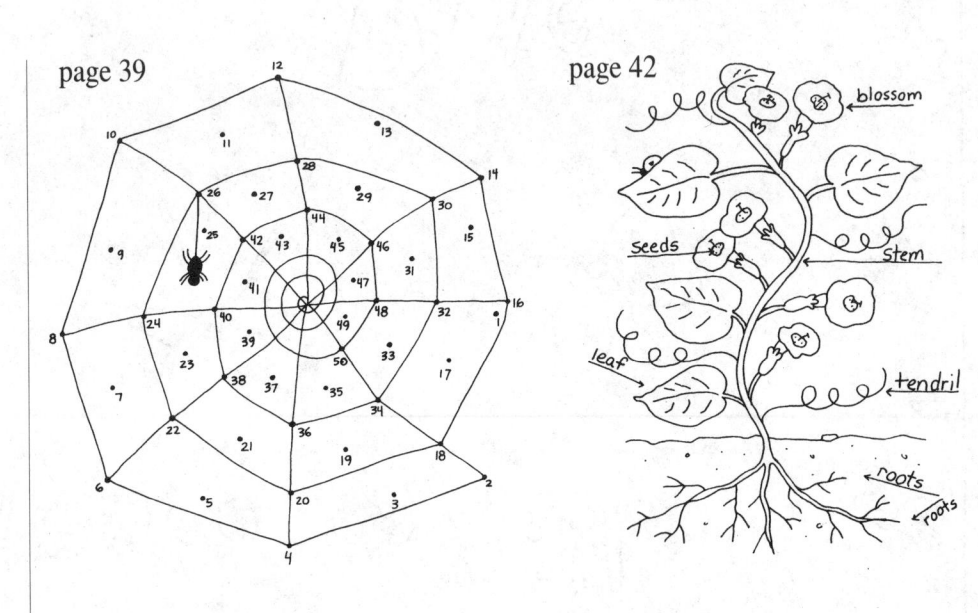

page 42

(plant diagram with labels: blossom, stem, seeds, leaf, tendril, roots, roots)

page 43

1. F	6. T
2. T	7. T
3. T	8. T
4. F	9. T
5. T	10. T

page 53

1. forest	6. grasslands
2. ocean	7. ocean
3. rainforest	8. grasslands
4. ocean	9. forest
5. forest	10. desert

page 56

```
H U M I D G O F W A F
O M C L O U D S O R O
T L S L E E Y N N U S
O I C W I N D Y S M L
L A Y L L I H C P T E
C H C L O A S U N N E
E R U T A R E P M E T
```

page 60

Mercury—0	Mars—2	Uranus—15
Venus—0	Jupiter—16	Neptune—2
Earth—1	Saturn—23	Pluto—0